Stoicism for New Parents

Calm Parenting Through Stoic Principles

Lane Adams

Copyright © 2024 by Lane Adams

All rights reserved. No part of this publication may be reproduced, stored or transmitted in any form or by any means, electronic, mechanical, photocopying, recording, scanning, or otherwise without written permission from the publisher. It is illegal to copy this book, post it to a website, or distribute it by any other means without permission.

Table Of Content

Introduction — 5
    The Challenges of Modern Parenting — 5
    Why Stoicism Matters for New Parents — 6

Chapter 1 — 9
    Understanding Stoicism: A Parent's Guide — 9
        The Core Principles of Stoicism — 9
        How Stoicism Applies to Parenthood — 11

Chapter 2 — 15
    Embracing Calm Amid Chaos — 15
        Managing Stress and Overwhelm — 15
        Responding Instead of Reacting — 17

Chapter 3 — 23
    Building Resilience in Parenthood — 23
        Accepting What You Can and Cannot Control — 23
        Cultivating Inner Strength — 25

Chapter 4 — 29
    Patience: The Stoic Superpower — 29
        Navigating Sleepless Nights and Tantrums — 29
        Staying Present During Difficult Moments — 31

Chapter 5 — 35
    Fostering Gratitude and Joy — 35
        Finding Beauty in Everyday Parenting — 35
        The Role of Reflection in Gratitude — 37

Chapter 6 — 41
    Teaching Stoicism to Your Children — 41

Leading by Example	41
Instilling Resilience and Emotional Strength	43
Chapter 7	**47**
Strengthening Family Bonds Through Stoicism	47
Communication Rooted in Compassion	47
Building a Harmonious Home Environment	49
Chapter 8	**53**
Overcoming Guilt and Perfectionism	53
Accepting Imperfection in Parenting	53
Letting Go of Unrealistic Expectations	55
Chapter 9	**59**
Stoic Practices for Everyday Parenting	59
Daily Exercises to Stay Grounded	59
Journaling for Reflection and Growth	62
Conclusion	**67**
The Journey of Stoic Parenting	67
Embracing the Long View	67
Continuing the Practice Beyond Early Parenthood	69

Introduction

The Challenges of Modern Parenting

Parenting has always been a profound and rewarding journey, but modern times have introduced complexities that previous generations could scarcely imagine. Today's parents face an overwhelming array of expectations, both from themselves and society. From the moment a child is born, parents are inundated with advice, opinions, and pressures—all of which are amplified by the pervasive presence of social media. Parenting milestones are now publicly scrutinized, compared, and celebrated, creating a digital landscape where perfection seems not only possible but required.

Add to this the practical challenges: balancing demanding careers with family life, navigating financial strains, and ensuring children receive the best education and opportunities. These pressures create a storm of anxiety, guilt, and self-doubt that can make even the most joyful moments feel fleeting or overshadowed.

Modern parents are also contending with the rapid pace of technological advancement and its impact on children. Screen time debates, online safety concerns, and the fear of raising children in a hyperconnected world weigh heavily on the minds of many. The result is a constant tension between wanting to do everything "right" and grappling with the realization that perfection is unattainable.

Amid these challenges, the emotional toll can be significant. Sleepless nights, tantrums, and the sheer unpredictability of raising a child can test anyone's patience. Moments of joy can quickly be replaced by frustration, leaving parents feeling isolated and exhausted. In this whirlwind, it's easy to lose sight of the bigger picture: the profound love and connection that make parenting such a meaningful experience.

Why Stoicism Matters for New Parents

Enter Stoicism, an ancient philosophy with timeless wisdom that feels tailor-made for the modern parenting journey. Rooted in the teachings of thinkers like Epictetus, Seneca, and Marcus Aurelius, Stoicism offers practical tools for navigating life's inevitable challenges with grace, resilience, and clarity. While its origins lie in ancient Greece and Rome, the principles of Stoicism are remarkably applicable to the highs and lows of parenting today.

At its core, Stoicism teaches us to focus on what we can control and to accept what we cannot. For parents, this is a revelation. How often do we fret over things beyond our influence—a baby's unpredictable sleep patterns, a toddler's public meltdown, or the opinions of others about our parenting choices? Stoicism encourages us to shift our energy from worrying about these external factors to cultivating inner strength and wisdom. By doing so, we can approach each parenting challenge with a calmer, more centered mindset.

Stoicism also emphasizes the importance of living in alignment with our values, a lesson that resonates deeply for parents striving to raise children with integrity and purpose. In a world that often prioritizes superficial achievements, Stoicism reminds us to focus on the character traits we wish to instill in our children: kindness, resilience, patience, and gratitude. It's not about raising perfect children but guiding them to become thoughtful and compassionate individuals.

Perhaps one of Stoicism's greatest gifts to new parents is its emphasis on presence. Parenting is full of fleeting moments—a baby's first smile, a child's curious questions, or the quiet comfort of a bedtime story. Stoicism teaches us to savor these experiences fully, without being distracted by regrets about the past or anxieties about the future. By grounding ourselves in the present, we can find joy and meaning even in the most mundane tasks.

Another powerful aspect of Stoicism is its approach to emotions. While Stoicism is sometimes misunderstood as advocating emotional suppression, it actually teaches us to acknowledge and understand our feelings without being ruled by them. This is particularly valuable for parents, who often experience a whirlwind of emotions, from elation to frustration, within the span of a single day. By practicing emotional resilience, we can respond to parenting challenges with greater clarity and patience.

Stoicism also offers solace for the inevitable mistakes and missteps of parenting. No parent is perfect, and no child expects perfection. Through Stoicism, we learn to forgive ourselves and embrace the imperfections of our journey. This self-compassion not only benefits us but also models a healthy and realistic approach to life for our children.

In a world that often feels chaotic and unpredictable, Stoicism serves as an anchor for new parents. It provides a framework for navigating the complexities of modern parenting with a sense of purpose, balance, and inner peace. By embracing Stoic principles, parents can cultivate a mindset that not only benefits their own well-being but also enriches their relationship with their children.

The path of parenthood is as challenging as it is beautiful, and Stoicism offers a guiding light through the turbulence. It reminds us that while we cannot control every aspect of our children's lives or shield them from every hardship, we can control how we show up for them—with patience, presence, and unwavering love. This is the essence of Stoic parenting and the foundation for a fulfilling and harmonious family life.

Chapter 1

Understanding Stoicism: A Parent's Guide

The Core Principles of Stoicism

Stoicism is a philosophy born in ancient Greece and Rome, yet its timeless principles hold profound relevance for modern life, particularly for parents navigating the challenges of raising children. At its heart, Stoicism is a practical guide to living a life of virtue, resilience, and tranquility, even amidst adversity. Understanding its core principles is the first step in applying its wisdom to the transformative journey of parenthood.

One of the most fundamental tenets of Stoicism is the distinction between what we can control and what we cannot. According to the Stoics, true peace comes from focusing our energy on what lies within our sphere of influence: our thoughts, actions, and attitudes. Conversely, we must learn to accept external events beyond our control, such as the behavior of others, unforeseen challenges, or even the inevitable ups and downs of parenting. For parents, this principle offers a liberating perspective, freeing us from the futile effort of trying to micromanage every aspect of our child's life.

Another cornerstone of Stoicism is the pursuit of virtue, which the Stoics regarded as the highest good. Virtue, in this context, is not about moral perfection but about striving to embody qualities like wisdom, courage, justice, and self-discipline. For parents, cultivating these virtues can serve as a compass, guiding decisions and actions in the face of parenting's many dilemmas. Wisdom helps us discern the best course of action, courage enables us to face challenges with grace, justice reminds us to treat our children and others fairly, and self-discipline ensures we remain patient and composed.

Stoicism also emphasizes the importance of aligning our lives with nature. This doesn't mean retreating into the wilderness but rather living in harmony with the natural order of things. For parents, this principle encourages us to accept the developmental stages and individual temperaments of our children without resistance. It invites us to nurture them in ways that align with their unique needs and strengths, rather than imposing rigid expectations.

Equanimity, or a state of inner calm, is another key Stoic principle. Life is unpredictable, and parenting is no exception. The Stoics teach that by cultivating a mindset of equanimity, we can remain composed and grounded regardless of external circumstances. This doesn't mean suppressing emotions but rather managing them in a way that allows us to respond thoughtfully instead of reacting impulsively.

Finally, Stoicism encourages the practice of mindfulness and reflection. The Stoics believed in examining their thoughts and actions regularly to ensure they were living in alignment with their values. For parents, this practice can be transformative, offering moments of clarity amidst the chaos of daily life. Reflection allows us to celebrate our successes, learn from our mistakes, and approach each day with renewed intention.

How Stoicism Applies to Parenthood

Parenthood is a profound journey that challenges us in ways we never imagined. It's a role that demands patience, resilience, and unwavering love, often in the face of sleepless nights, toddler tantrums, and the constant pull of competing responsibilities. Stoicism provides a framework for navigating these challenges with grace and purpose, transforming not only how we parent but also how we grow as individuals.

The principle of focusing on what we can control is particularly powerful for parents. Many aspects of raising a child are beyond our control—their moods, their choices, and even their health at times. Instead of succumbing to frustration or anxiety over these uncertainties, Stoicism teaches us to shift our energy to what we can influence: creating a loving environment, modeling positive behavior, and responding to challenges with patience and wisdom. This mindset not only reduces stress but also fosters a sense of empowerment, reminding us that our efforts, however small, have a meaningful impact.

Another way Stoicism applies to parenthood is through its emphasis on virtue. Raising children is as much about shaping their character as it is about meeting their physical and emotional needs. By embodying virtues like patience, kindness, and honesty, we provide a living example for our children to follow. When we lose our temper or make mistakes, Stoicism reminds us to approach ourselves with compassion, using these moments as opportunities for growth rather than sources of guilt.

The Stoic principle of aligning with nature offers profound insights into parenting. Every child is unique, with their own strengths, challenges, and developmental timeline. Instead of resisting or trying to mold our children into preconceived ideals, Stoicism encourages us to embrace their individuality and nurture their growth in alignment with their natural tendencies. This approach fosters a deeper connection and a more harmonious parent-child relationship.

Equanimity is another Stoic principle that resonates deeply with parenting. Children are unpredictable, and even the best-laid plans can be upended by a sudden meltdown or an unexpected illness. Cultivating equanimity helps us remain calm and composed in the face of these disruptions, enabling us to respond with empathy and understanding rather than frustration. This inner calm not only benefits us but also creates a sense of security for our children, who often look to us for cues on how to navigate life's uncertainties.

Stoicism's approach to emotions is particularly valuable for parents. While it's natural to feel overwhelmed or frustrated at times, Stoicism teaches us to acknowledge these emotions without letting them dictate our actions. By practicing emotional resilience, we can respond to parenting challenges with greater clarity and intention. For example, instead of reacting impulsively to a toddler's tantrum, we can pause, take a deep breath, and address the situation with patience and empathy.

Reflection is another Stoic practice that holds great value for parents. Taking time to reflect on our parenting journey allows us to celebrate our successes, learn from our mistakes, and set intentions for the future. This practice can be as simple as journaling about the day's challenges and triumphs or taking a moment before bed to express gratitude for the joys of parenthood. Reflection not only helps us grow as parents but also deepens our appreciation for the fleeting moments that make this journey so meaningful.

Stoicism also offers a perspective on failure and imperfection that is particularly comforting for parents. No one gets it right all the time, and parenting is no exception. The Stoics remind us that mistakes are opportunities for growth, both for us and our children. By approaching our missteps with humility and a commitment to learn, we model resilience and self-compassion for our children, teaching them that it's okay to stumble as long as we keep moving forward.

At its core, Stoicism is about living with intention and aligning our actions with our values. For parents, this means prioritizing what truly matters: nurturing our children's well-being, fostering their growth, and building strong family connections. It's about finding meaning and joy in the everyday moments, from bedtime stories to shared laughter, and approaching each challenge as an opportunity to grow together.

Parenthood is a journey filled with uncertainty, joy, and profound love. Stoicism provides a compass to navigate this journey with grace, resilience, and clarity. By embracing its principles, we can not only become better parents but also discover deeper meaning and fulfillment in the remarkable adventure of raising children.

Chapter 2

Embracing Calm Amid Chaos

Managing Stress and Overwhelm

Parenthood often feels like an intricate balancing act, with countless responsibilities pulling parents in different directions. From managing daily routines to meeting the emotional needs of children, the sheer volume of tasks can be overwhelming. Stress becomes a constant companion, and without the right tools, it can erode the joy of parenting. Understanding how to manage stress and overwhelm is not just essential for parents—it's transformative.

Stress in parenting is inevitable, but it doesn't have to control you. One of the foundational lessons of Stoicism is the practice of distinguishing between what you can control and what you cannot. Many stressors in parenting fall into the latter category: a baby's sleepless nights, an unexpected tantrum, or even external judgments about your parenting choices. While these events can feel frustrating or disheartening, Stoicism invites parents to redirect their energy. Instead of fixating on the uncontrollable, focus on your own actions, attitudes, and responses. This mental shift can reduce the emotional weight of stress and create a greater sense of agency.

Another vital practice is reframing the way you perceive challenges. Instead of viewing stress as an enemy, consider it an opportunity for growth. Every sleepless night or chaotic morning is a chance to cultivate patience, resilience, and empathy. Stoicism teaches that adversity is not something to be avoided but embraced as a teacher. By shifting your perspective, you can find meaning in even the most challenging moments of parenting.

Practical tools for managing stress are equally important. Mindfulness is a cornerstone of both Stoic philosophy and modern approaches to stress management. Taking a few moments each day to center yourself, whether through deep breathing, meditation, or simply observing your surroundings, can help you maintain calm amidst chaos. These practices ground you in the present moment, where stress often loses its grip.

Another powerful tool is creating routines that promote stability and predictability. While life with children is inherently unpredictable, establishing rituals—such as family meals, bedtime routines, or weekly check-ins—can create anchors of calm in an otherwise hectic environment. These routines don't just benefit parents; they provide children with a sense of security and consistency that supports their emotional well-being.

Equally important is acknowledging your limits and seeking support. Parenting is not a solo endeavor, and trying to handle everything on your own can lead to burnout. Whether it's leaning on a partner, family member, or trusted friend, sharing responsibilities can lighten the load and provide a much-needed sense of connection. Even small gestures, like asking for help with household chores or taking turns with bedtime duties, can make a significant difference.

Finally, self-compassion is essential for managing stress. It's easy to fall into the trap of self-criticism, especially when things don't go as planned. Stoicism teaches that mistakes and setbacks are part of the human experience. By extending kindness to yourself, you can release the unrealistic expectation of perfection and create space for growth and learning. Remember, calmness is not about eliminating stress but about navigating it with grace and intention.

Responding Instead of Reacting

Parenting is an emotional journey, filled with moments of immense joy but also frustration, disappointment, and even anger. When a toddler throws a tantrum in the middle of a crowded store or a teenager challenges boundaries, the instinct to react impulsively can be powerful. However, Stoicism offers a different approach: responding instead of reacting.

Reacting is often driven by emotion and impulse. It's the sharp tone that escapes when you're frustrated or the hasty decision made in the heat of the moment. While natural, these reactions can escalate conflicts, create misunderstandings, and leave both parent and child feeling disconnected. Stoicism, however, encourages a deliberate and thoughtful response—one rooted in awareness and intention.

The first step in responding is cultivating self-awareness. Recognizing your emotional triggers and understanding how they influence your behavior is crucial. For instance, if you know that exhaustion makes you more irritable, you can take proactive steps to manage your energy levels or pause before addressing a challenging situation. This self-awareness allows you to interrupt reactive patterns and approach situations with greater clarity.

The practice of pausing is a powerful tool. When faced with a triggering moment, taking a few deep breaths or counting to ten can create the mental space needed to choose your response. This pause doesn't mean suppressing your feelings but rather giving yourself time to process them. By stepping back, you can consider the bigger picture and respond in a way that aligns with your values and goals as a parent.

Empathy is another cornerstone of responding. Stoicism emphasizes the importance of understanding others' perspectives, and this principle is especially relevant in parenting. When a child acts out, it's often a reflection of their unmet needs or struggles. Responding with empathy—acknowledging their feelings and seeking to understand the root cause—can de-escalate conflicts and strengthen your connection. For example, instead of reacting to a tantrum with frustration, you might say, "I see that you're upset. Can you tell me what's wrong?" This approach not only diffuses tension but also models emotional intelligence for your child.

Another aspect of responding is staying grounded in your role as a guide and mentor. As a parent, your actions and words shape how your child learns to navigate challenges and relationships. Responding thoughtfully means modeling the behaviors and attitudes you wish to instill. This doesn't mean suppressing your emotions but expressing them in ways that are constructive and respectful. For instance, if you're feeling frustrated, you might say, "I'm feeling overwhelmed right now, and I need a moment to think about how we can solve this together."

Stoicism also encourages the practice of focusing on solutions rather than dwelling on problems. When faced with a challenging situation, ask yourself, "What's the best way forward?" This forward-thinking mindset helps you move past the immediate emotional reaction and toward constructive action. For example, if your child refuses to do their homework, instead of reacting with anger, you might explore ways to make the task more manageable or engaging.

Reflection is another valuable tool for cultivating a responsive mindset. After a challenging interaction, take time to reflect on what happened, how you responded, and what you might do differently next time. This practice not only enhances your self-awareness but also helps you approach future situations with greater insight and intention. Reflection also teaches children that mistakes are opportunities for growth, fostering a family culture of learning and resilience.

Finally, responding instead of reacting requires patience—with your child, with the situation, and with yourself. Change takes time, and both you and your child are learning and growing together. Stoicism reminds us that progress is made one step at a time and that setbacks are an inevitable part of the journey. By approaching each challenge with patience and persistence, you can create a foundation of calm and connection that supports your family's well-being.

Embracing calm amid chaos is not about achieving a perfect state of peace but about cultivating the tools and mindset to navigate life's unpredictability with resilience and grace. By managing stress and overwhelm and learning to respond instead of react, you can create a parenting journey that is not only more peaceful but also deeply fulfilling.

Chapter 3

Building Resilience in Parenthood

Accepting What You Can and Cannot Control

Parenthood is a journey defined by unpredictability. From the moment a child enters the world, parents face countless situations that challenge their patience, understanding, and resourcefulness. The sleepless nights, sudden illnesses, unexpected tantrums, and evolving needs of a growing child can feel overwhelming. However, a significant aspect of resilience lies in accepting what you can and cannot control, a principle deeply rooted in Stoic philosophy.

One of the most liberating lessons of Stoicism is the distinction between what is within our control and what is not. This mindset is especially relevant for parents, who often find themselves striving to manage every detail of their children's lives. While it's natural to want the best for your child, attempting to control every outcome can lead to unnecessary stress and frustration. Recognizing and accepting the limits of your influence is not an admission of failure but an act of wisdom.

For parents, this means understanding that you cannot control your child's temperament, their every choice, or the external circumstances they will face. What you can control, however, is your own response to these factors. For instance, while you cannot prevent your child from feeling upset when things don't go their way, you can guide them in learning how to process and cope with disappointment. Similarly, while you cannot eliminate every potential risk or challenge they may encounter, you can equip them with the tools to navigate these situations with resilience.

This principle of acceptance also extends to managing expectations. Parenthood often comes with a set of preconceived notions about how things should be—from the milestones your child should achieve to the way family life should unfold. When reality deviates from these expectations, it can be a source of frustration or disappointment. Stoicism teaches that letting go of rigid expectations allows you to embrace the present moment and appreciate it for what it is. By focusing on what is, rather than what you think should be, you create space for gratitude and growth.

A practical way to cultivate acceptance is through mindfulness and reflection. Taking time to pause and evaluate your perspective can help you identify areas where you may be holding on too tightly to control. For example, if you find yourself feeling anxious about your child's performance in school or their behavior in social settings, ask yourself whether these outcomes are within your control. If they're not, consider how you can shift your energy toward supporting your child in ways that align with your values and their needs.

Acceptance also involves practicing self-compassion. As a parent, you will inevitably face moments where things don't go as planned—whether it's a missed opportunity, a misstep in discipline, or a day that feels completely derailed. Instead of dwelling on these moments, Stoicism encourages you to view them as opportunities to learn and grow. By extending grace to yourself, you model resilience and self-acceptance for your child, teaching them that imperfection is a natural part of life.

Resilience begins with accepting that life's challenges are not obstacles but opportunities for growth. By focusing on what you can control and releasing what you cannot, you free yourself from the weight of unnecessary stress and create a foundation of calm and clarity in your parenting journey.

Cultivating Inner Strength

Inner strength is the bedrock of resilience, and for parents, it's an essential quality that sustains you through the highs and lows of raising children. Cultivating inner strength involves developing a mindset and habits that empower you to face challenges with courage, grace, and perseverance. It's not about eliminating difficulties but about equipping yourself to navigate them with confidence and composure.

One of the first steps in building inner strength is fostering self-awareness. Understanding your own emotions, triggers, and coping mechanisms allows you to respond to challenges more effectively. For example, recognizing when you're feeling overwhelmed or stressed enables you to take proactive steps to care for yourself before these feelings escalate. This might involve taking a short break, seeking support, or simply acknowledging your emotions without judgment. Self-awareness not only strengthens your ability to manage stress but also enhances your capacity to connect with and support your child.

Stoicism emphasizes the importance of cultivating a strong sense of purpose and values. For parents, this means clarifying what truly matters to you in your parenting journey. Whether it's fostering kindness, encouraging curiosity, or building a sense of security, having a clear sense of purpose helps you stay grounded during challenging times. When faced with difficult decisions or moments of doubt, returning to your core values provides a guiding light that keeps you focused on what's most important.

Another key aspect of inner strength is practicing emotional regulation. Parenthood is filled with moments that can test your patience—from a toddler's refusal to cooperate to a teenager's rebellious streak. Learning to manage your emotions in these situations is a powerful way to model resilience for your child. Instead of reacting impulsively, take a moment to pause, breathe, and reflect on the best course of action. This not only helps you maintain composure but also teaches your child the value of thoughtful and measured responses.

Cultivating inner strength also involves embracing challenges as opportunities for growth. In Stoicism, obstacles are seen not as roadblocks but as stepping stones to greater resilience. When you encounter difficulties in parenting—whether it's navigating a tough conversation with your child or adjusting to a major life transition—approach these moments with curiosity and an open mind. Ask yourself, "What can I learn from this experience?" or "How can I grow as a parent and a person?" This mindset transforms challenges into valuable lessons that deepen your inner strength.

Gratitude is another practice that fosters inner strength. Taking time to appreciate the small joys of parenting—a child's laughter, a heartfelt hug, or a quiet moment of connection—can help you stay grounded and resilient during tough times. Gratitude shifts your focus from what's lacking to what's abundant, creating a sense of fulfillment and perspective that strengthens your resolve.

Building inner strength also involves creating a support network. Resilience doesn't mean doing it all alone; it's about recognizing when to seek help and surrounding yourself with people who uplift and support you.

Whether it's a partner, family member, friend, or parenting group, having a community to lean on can provide emotional and practical support during challenging times. Sharing your experiences and learning from others creates a sense of connection and reminds you that you're not alone in your journey.

Finally, inner strength is cultivated through consistent self-care. Taking time to nurture your physical, emotional, and mental well-being is not selfish—it's essential. Whether it's through regular exercise, enjoying a hobby, practicing mindfulness, or simply carving out moments of rest, prioritizing self-care replenishes your energy and strengthens your ability to show up fully for your child. Remember, resilience is not about pushing through exhaustion but about sustaining yourself for the long term.

Building resilience in parenthood is a journey of growth, self-discovery, and intentional effort. By accepting what you can and cannot control and cultivating inner strength, you create a foundation of stability and confidence that supports not only your own well-being but also the flourishing of your family. Resilience is not a destination but a practice, one that evolves and deepens as you embrace the challenges and joys of raising children.

Chapter 4

Patience: The Stoic Superpower

Navigating Sleepless Nights and Tantrums

Few experiences test a parent's patience as profoundly as sleepless nights and tantrums. These moments can feel unrelenting, pulling at the last threads of your energy and composure. Yet, they are also defining opportunities to cultivate patience, which lies at the heart of Stoic philosophy.

Sleepless nights often come with an overwhelming sense of exhaustion. Your body aches for rest, yet your child's needs demand your presence. In such moments, frustration can build, and irritation may creep in. But the Stoic parent understands that frustration stems not from the child's crying but from unmet expectations. Perhaps you expected a full night of sleep or a brief reprieve after a long day. Recognizing this disconnect helps reframe the situation. Your child's cries are not an affront to your peace but an expression of their vulnerability and need.

The Stoics teach us to anchor ourselves in what we can control. In these weary hours, you may not control your child's sleep patterns, but you can control how you respond. Instead of resisting the reality of sleepless nights, embrace them as part of your parenting journey. Consider them an opportunity to practice resilience and compassion. Even in exhaustion, you're building a foundation of trust with your child. They learn that you're there for them, no matter the hour, and this consistency fosters a sense of security that will benefit them for years to come.

Similarly, tantrums are a quintessential test of patience. When your child is overwhelmed with emotion, it's easy to feel triggered by their outburst. The noise, the disruption, and the public spectacle can all weigh heavily on a parent's nerves. However, tantrums are not about you; they are your child's way of processing emotions they cannot yet articulate. By shifting your perspective, you can respond with empathy rather than frustration.

Patience during a tantrum involves resisting the urge to meet chaos with chaos. Instead of reacting impulsively, pause and breathe. Let the storm pass while maintaining your composure. Your calm presence communicates to your child that emotions are natural and manageable. In these moments, patience is not passive but active. It's the deliberate choice to remain steady in the face of disruption, modeling emotional regulation for your child.

Practical tools can help you navigate these challenges. For example, during sleepless nights, create small rituals that bring you comfort—a warm drink, a soothing playlist, or a cozy corner for feeding or rocking your child. These rituals ground you and provide moments of respite. When dealing with tantrums, remember to lower yourself to your child's level, speak in a calm tone, and validate their feelings. These small actions can de-escalate the situation and reaffirm your connection.

Ultimately, sleepless nights and tantrums are temporary phases, even if they feel eternal in the moment. Patience transforms these trials into opportunities for growth—not just for your child but for you as well. By leaning into these moments with grace and determination, you embody the Stoic ideal of perseverance, turning challenges into a testament to your strength.

Staying Present During Difficult Moments

Parenting is a whirlwind of responsibilities, decisions, and emotions. Amid the constant demands, staying present can feel like an elusive goal. Yet, it is precisely during the difficult moments that presence becomes most crucial. The Stoics understood that life's true richness lies in the present moment—not in dwelling on the past or worrying about the future. For parents, this principle is a guiding light.

When a difficult moment arises, such as a conflict with your child or a challenging decision, the instinct might be to react quickly or seek distraction. However, Stoicism teaches the value of pausing and grounding yourself in the now. By bringing your full attention to the present, you gain clarity and the ability to respond thoughtfully rather than impulsively.

Staying present requires a conscious effort to let go of distractions and focus on what truly matters. For example, if your child is upset or acting out, put aside your phone, your to-do list, or the thoughts swirling in your mind. Sit with them, look them in the eye, and listen to their words or their cries. This act of presence communicates that they are seen and heard, which is often enough to begin diffusing tension. More importantly, it strengthens the bond between you, creating a sense of connection that endures beyond the difficult moment.

Presence also involves accepting the discomfort of the moment without resistance. Whether it's cleaning up a mess, handling a meltdown, or navigating a tough conversation, resisting the situation only amplifies stress. By contrast, leaning into the moment—fully experiencing it without judgment—can transform it. You might find humor in the absurdity of a chaotic dinner time or appreciation for the opportunity to teach your child a valuable lesson. Staying present allows you to find meaning even in mundane or challenging experiences.

The practice of mindfulness is a powerful tool for cultivating presence. Simple techniques, such as deep breathing or focusing on your senses, can anchor you in the here and now. For instance, when tensions run high, take a deep breath and notice the sensation of the air filling your lungs. Feel your feet on the ground and remind yourself that you are capable of handling this moment. These small practices help you remain centered and calm, even in the face of adversity.

Another aspect of staying present is recognizing the fleeting nature of parenting's challenges and joys. The sleepless nights, tantrums, and messy moments are all part of a larger tapestry that includes laughter, milestones, and moments of profound connection. By embracing each moment as it comes, you cultivate gratitude for the journey, even with its difficulties.

Presence also requires self-compassion. There will be times when you feel distracted, overwhelmed, or less patient than you'd like. Instead of criticizing yourself, acknowledge your humanity and recommit to being present. Each moment offers a fresh start, a new opportunity to show up for your child and yourself.

Difficult moments are inevitable in parenting, but they don't have to be moments of struggle. By staying present, you transform them into opportunities for connection, growth, and learning. Patience becomes not just an abstract ideal but a lived practice, one that shapes your relationship with your child and deepens your experience of parenthood. As the Stoics remind us, life is lived moment by moment, and each moment is a chance to embody the strength and grace of patience.

Chapter 5

Fostering Gratitude and Joy

Finding Beauty in Everyday Parenting

Parenthood is often portrayed as a series of grand milestones—first steps, first words, birthdays, and graduations. While these moments are undoubtedly precious, the true beauty of parenting lies in the quieter, everyday experiences that often go unnoticed. It's in the way your child's eyes light up when they discover something new, the sound of their laughter filling the room, or the simple joy of holding their hand during a walk. These seemingly small moments form the tapestry of parenthood, and finding gratitude in them is key to fostering joy.

It's easy to become so caught up in the busyness of daily life that these moments pass by without recognition. Between managing schedules, chores, and responsibilities, the mundane can overshadow the magical. Yet, when you pause to look closely, the beauty of these everyday interactions becomes evident. Consider the peaceful stillness of rocking your baby to sleep or the pride in your child's face after they've accomplished something new. These moments are fleeting but hold immense value.

The Stoic principle of focusing on the present aligns perfectly with the practice of finding beauty in everyday parenting. By being fully present, you can immerse yourself in the richness of the moment. When your child reaches for your hand, instead of brushing it off as routine, recognize it as an act of trust and love. When they ask an endless string of questions, see it as a reflection of their curiosity and desire to connect with you. These moments are opportunities to deepen your bond and create lasting memories.

Gratitude is a powerful tool for shifting your perspective and uncovering the beauty in the everyday. A simple practice is to end each day by reflecting on three moments that brought you joy or gratitude. These could be as simple as a shared smile, a quiet moment of rest, or a funny story your child told. Over time, this practice trains your mind to seek out and appreciate these moments as they happen.

Another way to cultivate gratitude is to document the small, meaningful moments of parenting. Keep a journal where you jot down the sweet, funny, or touching things your child says or does. Not only does this practice help you savor these moments, but it also creates a treasure trove of memories to revisit when the challenges of parenting feel overwhelming.

Finding beauty in everyday parenting also involves reframing challenges as opportunities. When your child throws a tantrum, instead of focusing solely on the frustration, recognize it as a chance to teach them about emotions and coping. When they make a mess while trying to help, appreciate their enthusiasm and willingness to contribute. These moments, though imperfect, are opportunities for growth and connection.

The beauty of parenting is not in its perfection but in its authenticity. It's in the messy, chaotic, and unfiltered moments that you and your child grow together. By choosing to see these moments through a lens of gratitude, you transform them into sources of joy and fulfillment.

The Role of Reflection in Gratitude

Gratitude doesn't always come naturally, especially during the demanding moments of parenthood. It's easy to feel weighed down by exhaustion, stress, or self-doubt. This is where reflection becomes an invaluable practice. By taking the time to pause and look back, you gain a clearer perspective on the many gifts that parenthood brings, even in its challenges.

Reflection allows you to step out of the immediate demands of the moment and see the bigger picture. For example, a particularly tough day might feel overwhelming in the moment, but upon reflection, you might realize it was also filled with small victories and moments of connection. Perhaps you managed to soothe your child during a meltdown, or you shared a laugh despite the chaos. These moments might be easy to overlook in the heat of the moment, but reflection brings them into focus.

One effective way to incorporate reflection into your routine is through journaling. At the end of each day, take a few minutes to write down your thoughts and feelings about your parenting experiences. Focus on moments that brought you joy or taught you something valuable. Reflect on what went well and what you'd like to improve. Over time, this practice helps you recognize patterns of gratitude and growth in your parenting journey.

Stoicism emphasizes the importance of gratitude not as a fleeting feeling but as a deliberate practice. One of the ways Stoics cultivated gratitude was by imagining life without the things they held dear, a technique known as negative visualization. For parents, this might mean imagining what life would be like without the presence of their child's laughter, curiosity, or even the challenges that shape their bond. This exercise is not meant to induce sadness but to deepen appreciation for what you have in the present moment.

Reflection also helps you reframe challenges. For instance, if your child's behavior tested your patience, reflect on what the experience taught you. Perhaps it highlighted an area where you can grow as a parent or revealed something about your child's needs. Viewing challenges through the lens of gratitude doesn't minimize their difficulty but allows you to find meaning and value in them.

Another powerful form of reflection is sharing your thoughts and experiences with others. Talking to a partner, friend, or parenting group about your day can provide new perspectives and reinforce your sense of gratitude. Hearing others' stories and challenges can also remind you of the universal nature of parenting's ups and downs, fostering a sense of connection and solidarity.

Reflection is not just about looking back; it's also about setting intentions for the future. By identifying what you're grateful for and what brings you joy, you can consciously create more of those experiences. For example, if you've noticed that spending undistracted time with your child brings both of you happiness, you might make it a priority to incorporate more of those moments into your routine.

Parenthood is a journey of constant growth and learning, and reflection is a tool that helps you navigate it with grace and gratitude. It reminds you of the beauty in the ordinary, the lessons in the challenges, and the joy in the fleeting moments. By making reflection a regular practice, you deepen your appreciation for the incredible journey of raising a child and strengthen your ability to find joy even in the most demanding days.

Fostering gratitude and joy in parenthood is not about ignoring its difficulties but about embracing its fullness. By finding beauty in everyday moments and engaging in meaningful reflection, you cultivate a sense of gratitude that enriches both your experience and your relationship with your child. Gratitude becomes a wellspring of joy, resilience, and connection, transforming the journey of parenting into one of profound fulfillment.

Chapter 6

Teaching Stoicism to Your Children

Leading by Example

Children are keen observers, often absorbing lessons from what they see rather than what they are told. As a parent, teaching Stoicism to your children begins with embodying its principles in your daily life. When you practice patience, resilience, and emotional regulation, you provide a living example of the values you want to instill in them.

Leading by example is not about being a perfect parent but about showing your children how to navigate life's challenges with grace and composure. When setbacks occur, such as missing an important event or dealing with a family conflict, your response becomes a teaching moment. If you approach the situation with calmness and a focus on what you can control, your child observes how resilience works in action. Your ability to pause, assess, and respond thoughtfully becomes a model for their own behavior.

One of the most powerful ways to demonstrate Stoicism is through how you handle emotions. Children often struggle with understanding and regulating their feelings, and your response to your emotions provides a blueprint for them. When you're feeling overwhelmed, acknowledging your emotions and showing how you work through them—whether by taking a deep breath, reflecting, or stepping away to regain composure—teaches them that emotions are manageable and not something to fear or suppress.

Stoicism also emphasizes the importance of living according to values, and this is a concept children can grasp early on. When you prioritize honesty, kindness, and integrity in your actions, your child learns that these values are central to how you navigate the world. For example, keeping promises, even when inconvenient, demonstrates the importance of commitment. Apologizing when you're wrong shows humility and accountability. These small actions leave a lasting impression and help your child develop their moral compass.

Everyday situations provide countless opportunities to model Stoic principles. For instance, when plans don't go as expected—a canceled outing or a sudden change in routine—how you handle disappointment sets the tone for your child's reaction. If you show acceptance and adaptability, they're more likely to mirror that attitude. Similarly, when facing frustration, such as being stuck in traffic or dealing with a minor inconvenience, your ability to remain patient demonstrates the power of perspective and self-control.

Another key aspect of leading by example is showing gratitude and finding joy in the present moment. When you express appreciation for small, everyday blessings, your child learns to do the same. Gratitude fosters a positive outlook and helps them develop resilience by focusing on what they have rather than what they lack. Sharing moments of joy, whether through laughter, play, or quiet reflection, reinforces the value of presence and connection.

By consistently embodying Stoic principles, you create an environment where these values are not just taught but lived. Your actions become a silent yet powerful guide, shaping how your child approaches life's challenges and joys.

Instilling Resilience and Emotional Strength

Resilience and emotional strength are foundational to a child's ability to navigate the ups and downs of life. These qualities enable them to bounce back from setbacks, handle stress, and maintain a sense of balance in the face of adversity. Teaching these skills early helps them build a strong emotional foundation that will serve them throughout their lives.

Stoicism offers practical tools for fostering resilience in children. One of the most effective ways to start is by helping them differentiate between what they can and cannot control. This concept can be introduced in simple terms. For example, if your child is upset because it's raining and they can't play outside, you can explain that while they can't change the weather, they can choose how to spend their time indoors. Offering alternatives, such as playing a game or reading a book, helps them see how shifting focus to what they can control makes challenges more manageable.

Another important aspect of resilience is developing a growth mindset. Encourage your child to view mistakes and failures as opportunities for learning rather than as defining moments. When they struggle with a task, such as learning a new skill or completing a challenging assignment, praise their effort and perseverance rather than the outcome. Emphasizing progress over perfection teaches them that setbacks are a natural part of growth and not something to fear or avoid.

Emotional strength also involves understanding and managing feelings. Children often experience intense emotions but lack the tools to process them effectively. As a parent, you can help by validating their feelings and guiding them toward constructive ways of coping. For example, if your child is angry, acknowledge their frustration and encourage them to express it through words, drawing, or physical activity. Providing a safe space for emotions helps them feel understood and equips them with strategies for self-regulation.

Stoicism emphasizes the importance of perspective, and this is a skill children can learn with guidance. When your child feels overwhelmed by a problem, help them put it into context. Ask questions like, "Will this matter a week from now?" or "What's one thing we can do to make this better?" These questions encourage them to step back and view the situation from a broader angle, reducing its emotional intensity.

Teaching resilience also involves encouraging independence and problem-solving. Allow your child to face age-appropriate challenges and make decisions on their own. While it's natural to want to shield them from discomfort, stepping back and letting them navigate difficulties builds confidence and self-reliance. Offer support and guidance, but resist the urge to solve every problem for them. When they succeed, celebrate their effort and determination. When they struggle, be there to provide reassurance and help them learn from the experience.

Modeling self-care is another way to instill emotional strength. When children see you taking time to rest, reflect, and recharge, they learn that self-care is an essential part of resilience. Encourage them to adopt their own self-care routines, whether it's spending time in nature, practicing mindfulness, or pursuing hobbies that bring them joy.

Lastly, fostering resilience and emotional strength requires patience and consistency. Children learn through repetition and reinforcement, so keep the lines of communication open and provide ongoing support as they navigate their emotions and challenges. Celebrate their progress and remind them that building resilience is a lifelong journey.

By teaching your children the principles of Stoicism—acceptance, perspective, and emotional regulation—you equip them with tools to face life's uncertainties with confidence and grace. These lessons not only prepare them for the future but also strengthen your bond, creating a foundation of trust, understanding, and mutual growth.

Chapter 7

Strengthening Family Bonds Through Stoicism

Communication Rooted in Compassion

Effective communication is the foundation of strong family bonds. When approached with compassion, communication becomes a tool for understanding, connection, and conflict resolution. In the context of Stoicism, compassionate communication means speaking and listening with intention, empathy, and respect. It's about creating a safe space where every family member feels heard and valued.

One of the core tenets of Stoic communication is the concept of responding rather than reacting. In moments of tension or disagreement, it can be easy to let emotions take over and respond impulsively. However, Stoicism teaches the importance of pausing, reflecting, and choosing words that align with your values. This approach not only de-escalates conflicts but also models healthy communication for your children.

For instance, if your child is upset or acting out, instead of reacting with frustration, try to understand the underlying cause. Ask questions like, "Can you tell me what's bothering you?" or "How can I help you feel better?" By showing empathy and validating their feelings, you teach them that their emotions are important and manageable. This creates a sense of trust and strengthens your bond.

Compassionate communication also involves active listening. This means giving your full attention to the person speaking, without interrupting or formulating your response while they're still talking. For children, knowing that they have your undivided attention reinforces their sense of worth and encourages them to express themselves openly. When they feel heard, they're more likely to listen in return, fostering a reciprocal relationship of respect.

For parents, it's equally important to express emotions and needs in a constructive way. Instead of using accusatory language, focus on "I" statements that convey your feelings without placing blame. For example, saying "I feel overwhelmed when the house is messy" is more effective and less confrontational than "You never help clean up." This approach reduces defensiveness and opens the door to collaboration and problem-solving.

Compassionate communication extends beyond resolving conflicts; it's also about building connections through positive interactions. Share your thoughts, experiences, and feelings with your family, and encourage them to do the same. Celebrate achievements, express gratitude, and engage in meaningful conversations. These moments of connection deepen your relationships and create a supportive family environment.

Teaching your children the art of compassionate communication equips them with essential life skills. They learn how to express themselves effectively, listen to others with empathy, and resolve conflicts constructively. By practicing these principles in your daily interactions, you set the stage for a household where understanding and mutual respect flourish.

Building a Harmonious Home Environment

A harmonious home environment is one where every family member feels safe, valued, and supported. Stoicism provides a framework for creating such an environment by emphasizing balance, cooperation, and intentional living. It's about cultivating a space where positivity thrives and challenges are approached with resilience and unity.

One of the key aspects of building harmony at home is setting clear expectations and boundaries. When everyone understands their roles and responsibilities, it reduces misunderstandings and fosters a sense of accountability. For example, establishing routines for chores, homework, and family time helps create structure and ensures that everyone contributes to the household's well-being. Involving children in this process teaches them the value of teamwork and shared responsibility.

Equally important is creating opportunities for connection and bonding. Regular family rituals, such as shared meals, game nights, or weekend outings, provide a platform for strengthening relationships and building lasting memories. These moments of togetherness create a sense of belonging and remind everyone of the support and love that exists within the family unit.

A harmonious home environment also requires managing conflicts in a constructive way. Disagreements are inevitable in any family, but how they are handled makes all the difference. Stoicism teaches that conflict is an opportunity for growth and understanding. When conflicts arise, approach them with patience and a focus on finding solutions rather than assigning blame. Encourage open dialogue where everyone's perspective is considered, and work together to resolve issues amicably.

Gratitude plays a significant role in fostering harmony at home. When family members regularly express appreciation for one another, it creates a positive and uplifting atmosphere. Simple gestures like thanking your partner for their support or acknowledging your child's efforts go a long way in building a culture of mutual respect and encouragement. Gratitude shifts the focus from what is lacking to what is abundant, reinforcing a sense of contentment and connection.

Another essential element of a harmonious home is maintaining a calm and peaceful energy. As a parent, your demeanor sets the tone for the household. When you approach challenges with composure and optimism, it creates a ripple effect that influences the entire family. Stoicism's emphasis on controlling what you can and accepting what you cannot helps you navigate the ups and downs of family life with grace.

Creating a harmonious home also involves prioritizing self-care for all family members. Encourage your children to explore activities that bring them joy and relaxation, whether it's reading, playing sports, or engaging in creative pursuits. Lead by example by taking time for your own self-care, demonstrating the importance of maintaining balance and well-being. When everyone's physical, emotional, and mental needs are met, the family as a whole becomes more resilient and harmonious.

Finally, fostering harmony at home requires an ongoing commitment to growth and adaptability. Families evolve over time, and so do their dynamics and needs. Be open to change and willing to adjust your approach as necessary. Regularly check in with your family to understand their needs, concerns, and aspirations. By staying attuned to one another, you create a home environment that is not only harmonious but also nurturing and empowering.

Strengthening family bonds through Stoicism is about more than addressing challenges; it's about cultivating an environment where love, respect, and understanding thrive. Through compassionate communication and a focus on harmony, you create a foundation that supports your family's growth and happiness. These principles not only enrich your relationships but also provide your children with the tools they need to build meaningful connections in their own lives.

Chapter 8

Overcoming Guilt and Perfectionism

Accepting Imperfection in Parenting

Parenting is often romanticized as a journey of endless joy, boundless patience, and impeccable decision-making. However, the reality is far more complex. Each day brings unique challenges, and no parent can navigate them flawlessly. Accepting imperfection in parenting is not only a relief but also an essential step toward fostering a healthy family dynamic. Stoicism teaches us that perfection is an illusion and that embracing our humanity allows us to focus on what truly matters.

The pressure to be the "perfect parent" comes from various sources: societal norms, social media, well-meaning advice, and even our own upbringing. These influences can create an idealized version of parenting that is impossible to achieve. When we fall short of these expectations, feelings of guilt and inadequacy often follow. But Stoicism reminds us that we cannot control external perceptions or expectations—only our responses to them. By letting go of the need to meet an unattainable standard, we free ourselves to be present and authentic in our parenting journey.

Accepting imperfection begins with acknowledging that mistakes are a natural part of growth—for both parents and children. Every misstep is an opportunity to learn, adapt, and improve. For example, losing your temper during a stressful moment doesn't define your worth as a parent; rather, it's an opportunity to reflect and find better ways to manage similar situations in the future. Modeling this approach to mistakes shows your children that it's okay to be imperfect and that growth is a lifelong process.

Perfectionism can also manifest as an overwhelming desire to shield children from discomfort or failure. While this instinct comes from a place of love, it can inadvertently prevent children from developing resilience and problem-solving skills. Embracing imperfection means recognizing that your role as a parent is not to eliminate challenges but to guide your children through them. Allowing your child to experience frustration, disappointment, or even failure equips them with the tools they need to navigate the complexities of life.

It's also important to remember that each child is unique, and there is no one-size-fits-all approach to parenting. What works for one child may not work for another, and that's perfectly okay. Accepting imperfection involves being flexible and open to adjusting your methods as you learn more about your child's needs and personality.

This adaptability is a strength, not a weakness, and it demonstrates your commitment to meeting your child where they are.

Practicing self-compassion is a powerful way to counteract the effects of perfectionism. Treat yourself with the same kindness and understanding that you would offer a close friend. Remind yourself that parenting is a journey filled with trial and error and that your worth is not determined by your ability to meet arbitrary standards. Celebrate your efforts, no matter how small, and recognize the love and care that drive your actions.

Accepting imperfection doesn't mean settling for mediocrity; rather, it means focusing on what truly matters: creating a loving, supportive environment where your child can thrive. By letting go of the pursuit of perfection, you create space for connection, growth, and joy—for both you and your child.

Letting Go of Unrealistic Expectations

Unrealistic expectations can be a significant source of stress and guilt for parents. Whether they stem from personal aspirations, societal pressures, or comparisons with others, these expectations often set us up for disappointment and self-criticism. Letting go of these unattainable standards is a liberating process that allows us to approach parenting with greater clarity and purpose.

Many parents enter the journey with preconceived notions about what parenting should look like. These expectations might include always knowing the right answer, maintaining a perfectly organized home, or raising a child who excels in every area. While these goals may seem admirable, they are often unrealistic and fail to account for the unpredictability of life. Stoicism teaches us to focus on what is within our control and to release the rest. Applying this principle to parenting helps us reframe our expectations in a way that is both realistic and empowering.

One common source of unrealistic expectations is the comparison trap. Social media, in particular, presents a curated version of parenting that highlights only the best moments while obscuring the challenges. It's easy to feel inadequate when comparing your own messy, imperfect reality to the polished images of others. However, Stoicism reminds us that appearances can be deceiving and that true fulfillment comes from within. By shifting your focus from external validation to internal values, you can break free from the cycle of comparison and find contentment in your unique parenting journey.

Letting go of unrealistic expectations also involves recognizing that parenting is not about achieving specific outcomes but about nurturing your child's growth and well-being. For example, it's natural to hope that your child will excel academically, athletically, or socially. However, placing too much emphasis on these outcomes can create unnecessary pressure for both you and your child. Instead, focus on fostering qualities like curiosity, kindness, and resilience—traits that will serve them well regardless of their achievements.

It's equally important to set realistic expectations for yourself as a parent. You are not a superhero, and it's okay to ask for help, take breaks, or prioritize self-care. Acknowledging your limitations doesn't make you less capable; it makes you human. When you give yourself permission to rest and recharge, you're better equipped to show up for your family with patience and presence.

Reevaluating your expectations also involves embracing the unpredictability of parenting. Children are constantly growing and changing, and what works today may not work tomorrow. Instead of rigidly adhering to a specific plan, adopt a flexible mindset that allows you to adapt to new circumstances. This approach not only reduces stress but also helps you stay attuned to your child's evolving needs.

Practicing gratitude is another powerful way to counteract the effects of unrealistic expectations. Instead of focusing on what you think you're lacking, take time to appreciate the small, meaningful moments that make parenting worthwhile. Whether it's a shared laugh, a hug, or a quiet moment of connection, these experiences are the true rewards of parenting. Gratitude shifts your perspective and helps you find joy in the journey, even amidst its challenges.

Letting go of unrealistic expectations doesn't mean abandoning your hopes or lowering your standards. It means approaching parenting with a sense of balance and perspective. By focusing on what truly matters and releasing the need for perfection, you create an environment where both you and your child can thrive. This process is not about giving up but about embracing the freedom to parent authentically and wholeheartedly.

Chapter 9

Stoic Practices for Everyday Parenting

Daily Exercises to Stay Grounded

Parenting is a journey filled with unpredictability, challenges, and emotional highs and lows. Staying grounded amid the demands of daily life requires intentionality and discipline. Stoicism offers practical exercises that can help parents maintain their balance and focus on what truly matters, even in the midst of chaos. Incorporating these daily practices into your routine can transform your mindset and enhance your ability to navigate parenting with calm and confidence.

One foundational Stoic exercise is the practice of morning preparation. Before the day begins, take a few moments to center yourself and set your intentions. Reflect on the potential challenges that might arise and how you can respond to them with patience and wisdom. For example, you might anticipate a stressful morning routine or a difficult conversation with your child. By visualizing these scenarios and mentally rehearsing a calm, thoughtful response, you equip yourself to handle them with composure. This practice, often referred to as "premeditatio malorum" (the premeditation of evils), helps you approach your day with a sense of preparedness rather than reactivity.

Another powerful exercise is practicing mindfulness throughout the day. While Stoicism and mindfulness are distinct philosophies, they share common ground in emphasizing the importance of presence. As a parent, it can be easy to become overwhelmed by multitasking or distracted by future worries. Instead, make a conscious effort to fully engage in the present moment. Whether you're playing with your child, preparing meals, or handling bedtime routines, give your full attention to the task at hand. This focus not only enhances your connection with your child but also fosters a sense of inner peace.

Gratitude is another cornerstone of Stoic practice that can be particularly impactful for parents. Take time each day to reflect on the aspects of parenting that bring you joy and fulfillment. Perhaps it's the sound of your child's laughter, a moment of connection during storytime, or the satisfaction of seeing them learn and grow. By focusing on these positive experiences, you train your mind to appreciate the beauty in everyday life, even amidst challenges. Gratitude shifts your perspective and reminds you of the meaningful purpose behind your efforts as a parent.

Stoicism also emphasizes the importance of detachment from external outcomes. In the context of parenting, this means focusing on your efforts rather than fixating on results. For instance, you might encourage your child to be kind or disciplined, but their behavior is ultimately beyond your complete control. By practicing detachment, you free yourself from unnecessary frustration or disappointment. This mindset allows you to concentrate on what you can influence: modeling positive behavior, providing guidance, and creating a supportive environment.

Evening reflection is another invaluable Stoic exercise for parents. At the end of each day, set aside time to review your actions and decisions. Consider what went well, what challenges you faced, and how you might improve. This practice, known as "askesis" in Stoic tradition, fosters self-awareness and continuous growth. For example, if you lost your temper during a stressful moment, reflect on what triggered your reaction and how you could handle similar situations differently in the future. Evening reflection helps you identify patterns, celebrate progress, and approach the next day with renewed intention.

Breathing exercises are a simple yet effective way to stay grounded during moments of stress or overwhelm. When faced with a difficult situation, pause and take a few deep breaths. Focus on the sensation of your breath entering and leaving your body. This practice calms your nervous system, clears your mind, and allows you to respond thoughtfully rather than react impulsively. Teaching your child this technique can also equip them with a valuable tool for managing their own emotions.

Incorporating these daily Stoic exercises into your parenting routine doesn't require a significant time commitment. Small, consistent actions can have a profound impact on your mindset and overall well-being. By grounding yourself in Stoic principles, you create a foundation of resilience, patience, and clarity that supports both you and your family.

Journaling for Reflection and Growth

Journaling is a powerful tool for self-reflection and personal growth, making it an ideal practice for parents seeking to navigate the complexities of raising children with intention and wisdom. In Stoicism, journaling serves as a means to examine thoughts, clarify values, and track progress. For parents, it provides an opportunity to process emotions, gain perspective, and align daily actions with long-term goals.

One way to incorporate journaling into your routine is through morning intention-setting. Begin your day by writing down your priorities and aspirations as a parent. Reflect on the values you want to embody, such as patience, kindness, or perseverance. Consider any specific challenges you anticipate and how you plan to approach them. For example, if you're concerned about managing a busy schedule, you might write, "Today, I will focus on staying calm and present, even during moments of stress." This practice helps you start the day with clarity and purpose.

Gratitude journaling is another effective way to cultivate a positive mindset. Each evening, take a few moments to record the aspects of parenting for which you are thankful. These can range from significant milestones to small, everyday moments of connection. For instance, you might write about a heartfelt conversation with your child, a moment of shared laughter, or simply the privilege of watching them grow. Gratitude journaling shifts your focus from challenges to blessings, reinforcing a sense of appreciation and joy.

Self-reflection is a central theme in Stoic journaling. Use your journal to explore your thoughts, feelings, and reactions to various parenting situations. For example, if you found yourself frustrated during a difficult interaction, write about what triggered your emotions and how you responded. Ask yourself whether your reaction aligned with your values and how you might handle a similar situation differently in the future. This process fosters self-awareness and helps you identify areas for growth.

Another valuable journaling exercise is "negative visualization." In this practice, you reflect on potential challenges or setbacks that could arise and consider how you would cope with them. While this might seem counterintuitive, it can actually reduce anxiety and build resilience. For parents, this might involve imagining scenarios such as a sleepless night, a tantrum in public, or a missed milestone. By mentally rehearsing these situations, you prepare yourself to face them with equanimity and grace.

Journaling can also be a space for celebrating successes and milestones. Parenting is a demanding journey, and it's easy to overlook the progress you and your child have made. Take time to acknowledge your efforts, whether it's finding a creative solution to a problem, fostering a meaningful connection, or simply making it through a challenging day. Recording these moments reinforces your sense of accomplishment and provides encouragement for the future.

In addition to personal reflection, consider using your journal to document your child's growth and development. Write about their achievements, challenges, and unique personality traits. Capture the small details that might otherwise fade with time, such as the funny things they say, the books they love, or the milestones they reach. This not only creates a cherished record for the future but also deepens your appreciation for the present.

To make journaling a sustainable habit, find a routine that works for you. Some parents prefer to write in the quiet moments of the morning, while others find evening reflection more conducive to their schedule. The format can be as simple or elaborate as you like, from a dedicated notebook to a digital app. The key is consistency and authenticity; your journal is a space for honest, unfiltered expression.

Journaling is not about perfection or producing polished entries. It's about creating a space to explore your thoughts, clarify your intentions, and track your growth as a parent. Over time, this practice can help you develop a deeper understanding of yourself and your role, empowering you to approach parenting with confidence, resilience, and grace. By integrating journaling into your routine, you gain a powerful tool for navigating the challenges and joys of everyday parenting with Stoic wisdom.

Conclusion

The Journey of Stoic Parenting

Embracing the Long View

Parenting is a journey, not a destination. The challenges and triumphs you experience along the way are part of an ever-evolving story—one that demands patience, perspective, and an enduring commitment to growth. Stoicism, with its timeless wisdom, offers a framework for embracing the long view of parenting. It reminds us that our role as parents is not about immediate results but about fostering the kind of environment where growth, resilience, and character can flourish.

One of the central tenets of Stoicism is the understanding that progress is incremental. Just as a tree doesn't grow to its full height overnight, children develop slowly, shaped by the steady influence of their surroundings and the values modeled for them. As a parent, your daily efforts—even the seemingly small and mundane—contribute to this growth. Whether it's teaching kindness through example, guiding them through challenges with patience, or simply being present in their lives, these actions leave an indelible mark.

Looking at parenting through the lens of the long view also helps in managing expectations. Children, like all humans, are imperfect and will make mistakes. They will test boundaries, have moments of defiance, and struggle to grasp the lessons you aim to teach. But these moments are not failures; they are opportunities for learning and growth. Stoicism teaches us to accept what we cannot control and focus on our own actions and responses. By embodying this principle, you free yourself from undue frustration and cultivate a sense of calm resilience.

Taking the long view means recognizing that your role as a parent extends beyond the immediate challenges of today. It's about instilling values and virtues that will guide your child throughout their lives. These lessons may not always manifest immediately, but over time, the seeds you plant will take root. It's in the moments of reflection years from now—when your child demonstrates kindness, resilience, or wisdom—that you will see the lasting impact of your efforts.

The long view also reminds us to savor the journey. Parenthood is filled with fleeting moments of joy, connection, and wonder. From the first steps to heartfelt conversations, these experiences are precious and irreplaceable. Stoicism encourages us to remain present and fully engaged in these moments, appreciating them for the gifts they are. By focusing on the present while keeping the larger perspective in mind, you create a balance that enriches both your parenting and your personal growth.

Continuing the Practice Beyond Early Parenthood

The principles of Stoic parenting are not confined to the early years of raising a child. As your children grow, the challenges and dynamics of parenting will change, but the core values of Stoicism remain relevant. In fact, these principles can become even more vital as you navigate the complexities of adolescence, adulthood, and beyond.

As your children grow older, the nature of your influence shifts. During their younger years, you play a more directive role, guiding them through the basics of behavior, learning, and social interaction. But as they gain independence, your role transitions to that of a mentor and supporter. Stoicism equips you with the tools to embrace this change with grace. By focusing on leading by example, you continue to inspire and guide your children through your actions and values.

Adolescence, in particular, can be a time of turbulence and uncertainty. Teenagers are navigating their own identity, facing external pressures, and learning to make decisions on their own. As a parent, it's natural to feel a mix of concern and pride during this phase. Stoicism reminds us to approach these challenges with patience and understanding. Instead of trying to control every aspect of their lives, focus on providing a steady presence and a safe space for them to explore and grow.

The principle of accepting what you can and cannot control becomes especially poignant during this stage. You cannot shield your child from every difficulty or prevent them from making mistakes, but you can equip them with the tools to face adversity with courage and resilience. By practicing detachment from outcomes and trusting in the foundation you've built, you allow your child the freedom to learn and grow.

As your children transition into adulthood, the lessons of Stoicism continue to guide your relationship. While your role as a parent may evolve, your influence remains significant. Adult children still look to their parents for wisdom, support, and a model of how to navigate life's challenges. By continuing to embody Stoic principles, you provide a source of stability and inspiration for them, even as they forge their own paths.

Moreover, Stoicism teaches that parenting is not only about what you give to your children but also about what you learn from the experience. Parenthood is a profound journey of self-discovery, pushing you to grow in patience, empathy, and resilience. The challenges you face as a parent mirror the broader challenges of life, offering countless opportunities to practice and refine your Stoic principles. By remaining committed to this practice, you continue to grow alongside your children.

Another important aspect of continuing Stoic parenting is fostering an enduring sense of gratitude. As your children grow and develop lives of their own, it's easy to focus on what has changed or what you may miss about their younger years. Stoicism encourages us to focus on the present and appreciate each phase of life for what it offers. Whether it's celebrating their achievements, cherishing moments of connection, or simply appreciating the journey you've shared, gratitude helps you remain grounded and fulfilled.

Continuing the practice of Stoicism beyond early parenthood also means embracing the idea of lifelong learning. Just as your children are constantly growing and evolving, so too are you. Each stage of parenthood presents new challenges and opportunities for growth. By remaining open to learning and adapting, you not only become a better parent but also a more resilient and fulfilled individual.

Finally, Stoicism teaches us that the journey of parenting is never truly over. Even as your children grow independent, the lessons you've shared and the values you've instilled continue to ripple through their lives and the lives of those they touch. In this sense, the impact of Stoic parenting extends far beyond your immediate family. By raising resilient, compassionate, and thoughtful individuals, you contribute to a legacy of positive change in the world.

The journey of Stoic parenting is one of constant growth, reflection, and renewal. It's a practice that transcends the challenges of any particular moment and focuses on the enduring values that guide us through life. By embracing the long view and continuing the practice of Stoicism beyond the early years of parenthood, you create a foundation of strength, wisdom, and love that supports both you and your children for a lifetime.